THE
GENERATIONS
OF
NOAH

The Generations

of

Noah

by
Joseph Nathan Smith

Copyright © 2008 by
Joseph Nathan Smith

All Rights Reserved

Printed in the United States of America

Library of Congress Control Number: 2007905292

ISBN: 978-0-6151-9309-0

All Biblical references are from the public domain King James Version of the Bible. In every case, whether Biblical or not, each reference shows its source. Although none of the referenced words have been changed, some of the words have bold typing added.

Genesis 6:9-10

[9]These *are* the generations of Noah: Noah was a just man *and* perfect in his generations, *and* Noah walked with God. [10]And Noah begat three sons, Shem, Ham, and Japheth.

PREFACE

According to the Bible, Noah was born six hundred years before the great flood. Furthermore, this flood devastated the entire globe and every person was killed except Noah and his family. They survived because God saved them. After the flood Noah's descendants reproduced. Noah's sons and their wives had children. Their children matured and had children. Those children had children, and the process continued. Accordingly, the population of the world grew exponentially.

Exponential growth is amazing. Most people have probably heard the story of the boy who was asked to decide how he would be paid for a daily chore, which would last thirty days. He could be paid five dollars a day, or he could be paid one penny the first day and each day afterward his pay would double. The five dollars a day was tempting to him because $150 dollars was a very large amount of money to him. However, he chose the plan that doubled his pay each day. The first day he was paid one cent. The second day he was paid two cents. The third day he was paid four cents. The pay continued to double until the thirtieth day. Amazingly, on the last day he was paid $5,368,709.12!

Populations, whether of people or animals or bacteria, increase the same way. They increase in number exponentially. That is, the amount of the increase is dependent on the amount present. In the case of the boy, he didn't have much at the start so the increase was not much. However, near the end the amount was large and so the increase was large. This kind of growth process is well understood and can be expressed mathematically.

According to the Bible, a flood, which occurred only a few thousand years ago, decimated the population of the Earth and only Noah's family survived. That family was composed of Noah and his wife, and Noah's three sons and their wives. This Biblical declaration is a difficult concept to ponder, because at that point in time only eight people were alive on the entire planet Earth. Additionally, the Bible states that Noah's sons and their wives, a total of six people, were the progenitors of all subsequent human life. Could only six people who lived about four thousand years ago be solely responsible for the twenty-first century's population of billions?

Some people get very emotional when answering this question. For them the answer is entangled in their beliefs about religion or science. Fortunately, the question can be answered without emotional entanglements. Mathematics provides the answer.

Although this message makes use of mathematics and specifically exponential equations, an understanding of higher mathematics is not required. A full appreciation of this message can still be gleaned by simply skipping the mathematical derivations. For those who can follow the mathematical derivations, they are provided in full context. For those who wish to skip the rigors of the mathematics, the parts which can be safely skipped are clearly marked.

May God bless your reading of these words.

CONTENTS

1. ALL THAT THE LORD HATH SAID 15
2. THE FACE OF ALL THE EARTH................................19
3. EIGHT SOULS...25
4. THE BIBLICAL DATE FOR NOAH'S FLOOD 33
5. WORLD POPULATION STATISTICS..........................37
6. THE CHALLENGE 49
7. EXPONENTIAL GROWTH 55
8. TEST FOR REASONABLENESS 71
9. TEST FROM 1AD TO 2007AD..................................79
10. TEST FROM 1750AD TO 2007AD 87
11. TEST FROM 1900AD TO 2007AD 95
12. TEST FROM 2000AD TO 2007AD 103
13. CONFIRMING THE WORD 111

1

A<small>LL</small> <small>THAT</small> <small>THE</small> L<small>ORD</small> H<small>ATH</small> S<small>AID</small>

God has provided information for the benefit of humanity. Much of that information is contained in the Holy Scriptures. From long ago the people of Earth have understood this fact.

> Exodus 24:7
>
> ⁷And he took **the book of the covenant**, and read in the audience of the people: and they said, **All that the LORD hath said** will we do, and be obedient.

The people knew that what God "said" was written in "the book" for universal inspection. God speaks through His Holy Scriptures.

Many, however, reject God's words. They believe that the Bible is full of fables which cannot be true because they cannot stand the test of modern investigation. Believing that no rigorous tests of the Bible's claims are possible, they simply dismiss them. Without such testing, they scoff at the Bible and refuse to take it seriously. For them the Bible is a book written by people limited to their own historical perspective. For them the Bible is not the word of the illimitable God.

For instance, the modern secular intellect rejects the very idea of Noah's flood. The skeptic chides, "How could all the people in the entire Earth, except for one family, have been killed by one flood event? Furthermore, how could the Earth's vast population have started from that one family only a few thousand years ago?" Others resolve their intellectual issues with Noah's flood by framing it in an allegory; and thereby, they deny its reality. Yet in the face of all such skepticism, the Bible confidently proclaims the verity of Noah's flood.

Can the skeptic's objections be tested? Can the world population numbers, as recorded in the Bible for the time of Noah's flood, be objectively tested for reasonableness?

The answer to this question is yes. The mathematics of population growth allows such a test to be accomplished objectively and logically.

Three steps will be employed in the testing process. The first step will be the determination of world population facts strictly from the Bible's account of Noah's flood. The second step will be the collection of modern world population numbers strictly from a secular perspective. The third step will be the analysis of the data. The analysis inherently involves the application of the mathematics of population growth. This three-step process will test the reasonableness of the Bible's population numbers growing to the secular population numbers in the time frame specified by the Bible. If a problem with the Bible's numbers exists, the mathematics will show it.

THE GENERATIONS OF NOAH

Can the Bible's claims withstand such an objective test?

2

The Face of All the Earth

God destroyed the Earth during the life of Noah because of unrestrained sin and widespread violence. All air-breathing land animals, except for Noah, his family, and all other animals on the ark, were destroyed in a worldwide flood.

> Genesis 6:13
>
> [13]And **God said** unto Noah, The **end of all flesh** is come before me; for **the earth is filled with violence** through them; and, behold, **I will destroy them with the earth**.
>
> Genesis 6:17-18
>
> [17]And, behold, **I, even I**, do bring a **flood of waters upon the earth**, to **destroy all flesh**, wherein *is* the breath of life, from **under heaven**; *and* **every thing that** *is* **in the earth shall die**. [18]But with thee will I establish my

THE GENERATIONS OF NOAH

covenant; and thou shalt come into the ark, thou, and thy sons, and thy wife, and thy sons' wives with thee.

These statements describing worldwide destruction are not based on a misperception by a human being with limited observational capabilities. God made these statements. God spoke these things to Noah. Noah didn't actually need to understand. God was in charge of this project. Unequivocally, God clearly stated that all the Earth would feel the effect of the flood. God repeatedly made it plain that the extent of the flood was worldwide and that He was in control. He said, "I, even I, do bring a flood of waters upon the earth, to destroy all flesh, wherein *is* the breath of life, from under heaven; *and* every thing that *is* in the earth shall die." This statement is very precise and it was made by God Himself. All air-breathing land animals on the Earth outside the ark were targeted for destruction. God determined the extent of the destruction and God executed His plan. None could escape the oversight of God.

THE FACE OF ALL THE EARTH

For those who might argue that God didn't mean the entire surface of the Earth, God made many additional statements countering that argument.

> Genesis 7:1-4
>
> ¹And **the LORD said** unto Noah, Come thou and all thy house into the ark; for thee have I seen righteous before me in this generation. ²Of every clean beast thou shalt take to thee by sevens, the male and his female: and of beasts that *are* not clean by two, the male and his female. ³Of fowls also of the air by sevens, the male and the female; **to keep seed alive upon the face of all the earth.** ⁴For yet seven days, and I will cause it to rain upon the earth forty days and forty nights; and **every living substance** that I have made will **I destroy from off the face of the earth.**

Unmistakably, God refers to "the face of all the earth." Again, God is speaking and He fully understands the extent and boundaries of the

THE GENERATIONS OF NOAH

Earth. When God says "all the earth," a person who respects God must believe He meant all the Earth. Yet, more evidence is provided.

> Genesis 7:17-20
>
> [17]And the flood was forty days **upon the earth**; and the waters increased, and bare up the ark, and it was lift up **above the earth**. [18]And the waters prevailed, and were increased greatly **upon the earth**; and the ark went upon the face of the waters. [19]And the waters prevailed exceedingly **upon the earth**; and **all the high hills, that *were* under the whole heaven, were covered**. [20]Fifteen cubits upward did the waters prevail; and **the mountains were covered.**

All the high hills under the whole heaven were covered by the flood waters. All the mountains were covered by the flood waters. These observations are from God's point of view. God clearly said that the extent of the flood was worldwide from His perspective. If a person cannot accept these plain words from God's own mouth, then the Bible is simply not relevant to that person.

However, God does not want any truth-seeking person to miss the point. Hence, the Bible provides more detail. A particularly important point involves God's promise to never again flood the Earth.

> Genesis 9:11
>
> [11]And I will establish my covenant with you; neither shall all flesh be cut off any more by the waters of a flood; **neither shall there any more be a flood to destroy the earth**.

Clearly, God promised that the Earth would not be destroyed again by flood. God Himself made this promise. If Noah's flood was not worldwide, then God's promise not to do it again has been violated repeatedly. Certainly, many local floods have occurred since Noah's day. In fact, many of these floods have been very destructive. If Noah's flood was a local flood, then God has broken His promise many times because a multitude of

THE GENERATIONS OF NOAH

devastating local floods have occurred in the last few thousand years. The flood caused by Hurricane Katrina in the Gulf of Mexico is but one example. Only if Noah's flood was global does God's promise make sense and remain valid.

3

EIGHT SOULS

The Bible clearly states that Noah's flood was worldwide; however, what does the Bible say about the number of people who survived this flood?

> Genesis 7:13-16
>
> ¹³In the selfsame day entered **Noah**, and **Shem**, and **Ham**, and **Japheth**, the sons of Noah, and **Noah's wife**, and the **three wives of his sons** with them, into the ark; ¹⁴They, and every beast after his kind, and all the cattle after their kind, and every creeping thing that creepeth upon the earth after his kind, and every fowl after his kind, every bird of every sort. ¹⁵And they went in unto Noah into the ark, two and two of all flesh, wherein *is* the breath of life. ¹⁶And they that went in, went in male and female of all flesh, as

THE GENERATIONS OF NOAH

God had commanded him: and the LORD shut him in.

God personally shut Noah, his wife, Noah's three sons, and their wives into the ark. The ark contained only eight human beings. What happened to all the people outside of the ark?

Genesis 7:21-23

[21]And **all flesh died that moved upon the earth**, both of fowl, and of cattle, and of beast, and of every creeping thing that creepeth **upon the earth**, and **every man**: [22]**All** in whose nostrils *was* the breath of life, of **all** that *was* in the dry *land*, died. [23]And **every living substance was destroyed** which was **upon the face of the ground**, both man, and cattle, and the creeping things, and the fowl of the heaven; and they were **destroyed from the earth**: and **Noah only** remained *alive*, **and they that** *were* **with him in the ark**.

EIGHT SOULS

If a person was not in the ark, that person was killed by the flood that enveloped the entire Earth. Only those in the ark survived. Therefore, the Bible provides the exact number of people on the entire planet Earth immediately after the flood. That number was eight.

To remove all doubts about what the Bible is communicating, it plainly states that Noah's sons were the progenitors of the entire population of the Earth. Noah had three sons and each son had one wife. Those sons and their wives repopulated the entire Earth after the flood.

> Genesis 9:18-19
>
> [18]And the sons of Noah, that went forth of the ark, were **Shem**, and **Ham**, and **Japheth**: and Ham is the father of Canaan. [19]These are the three sons of Noah: and **of them was the whole earth overspread**.

According to the Bible, from Noah's three sons the "whole earth" was overspread. Although eight

The Generations of Noah

people were present on the Earth immediately after the flood, only six people continued to have children. From Noah's three sons and their three wives, all of the subsequent population of the entire Earth was produced. Therefore, as attested by the Bible, everyone in the twenty-first century's world population is descended from these six people.

Not only does the Old Testament state that exactly eight people survived the flood, but the New Testament also reaffirms it.

> 1 Peter 3:18-20
>
> [18]For Christ also hath once suffered for sins, the just for the unjust, that he might bring us to God, being put to death in the flesh, but quickened by the Spirit: [19]By which also he went and preached unto the spirits in prison; [20]Which sometime were disobedient, when once the longsuffering of God waited **in the days of Noah**, while the ark was a preparing, wherein few, that is, **eight souls were saved** by water.

EIGHT SOULS

> 2 Peter 2:4-5
>
> ⁴For if God spared not the angels that sinned, but cast *them* down to hell, and delivered *them* into chains of darkness, to be reserved unto judgment; ⁵And spared not the **old world**, but saved **Noah the eighth** *person*, a preacher of righteousness, bringing in the flood upon the world of the ungodly...

Jesus, also, stated that in Noah's day all the people, who were not in the ark, were destroyed by the flood.

> Luke 17:26-27
>
> ²⁶And as it was **in the days of Noe**, so shall it be also in the days of the Son of man. ²⁷They did eat, they drank, they married wives, they were given in marriage, until the day that Noe entered into the ark, and the **flood** came, and **destroyed them all**.

The Bible's statements about Noah's flood and Noah's Ark are so clear and so numerous that two

The Generations of Noah

groups of people can be identified. The first group is composed of people who believe the Bible's simple statements, and the other group is composed of people who do not. Since Jesus is also making these statements, the first group, which believes the Bible, can be characterized as believing Jesus. Moreover, the second group, which does not believe the Bible, can be characterized as not believing Jesus.

The Bible's statements about Noah's flood and the Ark clearly polarize these two distinct groups: those who believe the statements and those who do not. Obviously, all Christians must defer to Christ. That's the whole point of being a Christian. Since Jesus plainly states that the flood destroyed "all" people not in the ark, no further discussion for them is required. The other group must be characterized as non-Christian because they have rejected the words of Christ and thereby rejected Him.

In summary, the Biblical account, in both the New and Old Testaments, states Noah's flood was worldwide and only eight people survived it: four men and four women. Of these eight people, six reproduced after the flood.

As a popular anecdote goes, an orphaned boy grew up and became very successful. Wanting to know about his family history, he hired a team of professionals to research his ancestors. He paid them $10,000 for their effort. However, when he saw what they had uncovered, he paid them $20,000 to cover it up again!

People often trace their ancestry for one reason or another, and some have discovered interesting facts about their family history. However, according to the Bible, if a modern-day person traces their blood-line back far enough, that journey will eventually get to the survivors of Noah's flood. Every human that has ever lived is descended from Adam and Eve, but everyone alive has a closer and more recent connection. Everyone on the face of the entire Earth is directly related by blood to

THE GENERATIONS OF NOAH

each other, because everyone is descended from Noah's family.

One more piece of information is required from the Bible. An approximate historical date for the occurrence of Noah's flood is needed. According to the Biblical record, what was the date for Noah's flood?

4

THE BIBLICAL DATE FOR NOAH'S FLOOD

Although the Bible does not directly give a date for Noah's flood, it gives enough information to determine it.

To that end, the Bible provides an abundance of information about the descendants of Adam. In fact, the genealogical record in Genesis chapter 5 provides a series of "begats" and the years between them. As an example, the following reference gives the first few descendants of Adam and the number of years separating them.

> Genesis 5:3-8
> ³And Adam lived an **hundred and thirty years**, and begat *a son* in his own likeness, after his image; and called his name Seth: ⁴And the days of Adam after he had begotten Seth were eight hundred years: and he begat sons and

The Generations of Noah

> daughters: ⁵And all the days that Adam lived were nine hundred and thirty years: and he died. ⁶And Seth lived an **hundred and five years**, and begat Enos: ⁷And Seth lived after he begat Enos eight hundred and seven years, and begat sons and daughters: ⁸And all the days of Seth were nine hundred and twelve years: and he died.

By tracking and summing the years from father to son, the number of years from Adam to Noah can be determined. When all the provided years are added, the time from the creation of Adam to the birth of Noah totals 1,056 years. In addition, the age of Noah when the flood started is provided.

> Genesis 7:6
>
> ⁶And **Noah *was* six hundred years old** when the flood of waters was upon the earth.

Since Noah was 600 years old at the beginning of the flood, Noah's flood occurred 1,656 years after the creation of Adam. However, an actual date for

THE BIBLICAL DATE FOR NOAH'S FLOOD

Noah's flood is needed, not just a relative position to another Biblical event.

Determining the actual date 1,656 years after Adam's creation is more difficult. However, amazingly and in opposition to popular secular opinion, a careful review of Biblical statements can provide an accurate date. Specifically, the book *Rest Unto The Land* has compiled statements from the Bible and shown that the date for Noah's flood is 2319BC (Rest Unto The Land, 2007, Joseph Nathan Smith, page 136). This date is consistent with other Biblical chronology and can serve as the Biblical reference point for the date of Noah's flood.

Even though other historical dates might be suggested for Noah's flood, most are within a few hundred years of 2319BC. As will be shown, an exact date is not required for the current discussion. Only a general bracket of time within a few hundred years is required. The referenced book is provided for those who want exacting justification for the date. In any case, most Biblical

THE GENERATIONS OF NOAH

scholars would concur that the Bible supports a flood date in the general range from 2100BC to 2500BC. Nevertheless, for this discussion 2319BC will be used as the reference date for Noah's flood.

The first step in the testing process is complete. All of the required world population data from the Bible has been collected. The next step involves the collection of world population data from a secular point of view.

5

W̲O̲R̲L̲D̲ ̲P̲O̲P̲U̲L̲A̲T̲I̲O̲N̲ ̲S̲T̲A̲T̲I̲S̲T̲I̲C̲S̲

World population numbers from the twentieth and twenty-first centuries have a general consensus of approval. That is, most people agree with them. However, world population numbers prior to the twentieth century do not have this attribute. In order to avoid any debate concerning which numbers are better with regard to political, social, religious, or scientific preferences, an average consensus of secular world population numbers will be used. This averaging process is necessary because no undisputed authority on world population statistics exists and exact numbers have never existed.

Most people seem to agree with world population numbers since 1950AD. This agreement probably exists because of the advent of computers and high speed communication equipment. These advancements seem to allow the task of a worldwide census to be accomplished reliably. Hence, no real controversy exists concerning these modern numbers. In addition, as the numbers get more and more modern, the general perception is that they get better and better. Moreover, if these numbers are rounded to the nearest 100 million, all genuine disagreement is removed. In fact, when reported world population numbers are restricted to the years after 1999AD and the numbers are rounded to the nearest 100 million, virtually all disagreement disappears.

For world population numbers prior to 1950AD, the general perception is that the numbers are not as reliable. Therefore, an additional strategy must be employed. In these cases, from all available estimates the maximum and minimum estimates will be averaged and then rounded to the nearest 100 million.

Collecting world population statistics, especially for specific dates hundreds or thousands of years in

WORLD POPULATION STATISTICS

the past, is a difficult task. It may be an easy task to count the number of people in a room, but it is extremely difficult to count the number of people in the entire Earth. However, a good counting method is not the only problem when dealing with estimates from the past. Imagine the difficulty if the counting problem was not just the number of people in a room, but instead the problem was the number of people in a room five years ago when no one was counting. Now imagine the immense difficultly of counting the number of people on the Earth 1,000 years ago! Furthermore, any world population count would only be a snapshot for a particular time since the number is always changing due to births and deaths. For these reasons mathematics is generally employed to determine the estimated population of the Earth at a particular time.

The secular world population information used in this discussion was taken from the United States Census Bureau. Their internet website has a collection of information not only about the United

THE GENERATIONS OF NOAH

States but about the world. In particular, statistics from 1AD to 1950AD can be found at the website **http://www.census.gov/ipc/www/worldhis.html**. Also, statistics after 1950AD can be found at **http://www.census.gov/ipc/www/idb/worldpop.html**. Since the information referenced from these websites is not copyrighted, they provided the basis for the secular world population data. This data was used to create a table of secular world population numbers for specific dates.

The dates chosen for the table were 1AD, 1750AD, 1900AD, 2000AD, and 2007AD. The first three dates were picked simply because they had the most world population estimates on the table found at the referenced web page. That is, these were the only dates that had at least nine of the eleven columns of data filled. For convenience the maximum and minimum estimates are also provided. Note that arbitrary dates such as 8AD or 213AD have no data at all. Note also, that the older data is sporadic and is only provided every 100 years or so. In contrast, from 1950AD forward the

WORLD POPULATION STATISTICS

average annual data is provided for each year and the average annual growth rate is also provided. The oldest year with a lot of estimates was 1AD. Apparently, the reliability of the historical data prior to the year 1AD is so low most are not willing to venture a guess at the population prior to it. The next oldest dates chosen with many estimates were 1750AD and 1900AD. For some reason a lot of estimates were available for these dates. Following the pattern, 2000AD was selected because it marks the turn of the next century. The year 2007AD was selected simply because it is the most recent estimate from the past.

From the referenced data an average consensus for a world population number must be determined for each selected date. For this discussion the method used to determine an average consensus is simple. All available estimates were used to arrive at a single world population number. However, by a strict definition, an actual average was not calculated. For 1AD the world population estimates ranged from 170 million to 400 million.

THE GENERATIONS OF NOAH

The average of these two numbers is 285 million. That number was rounded to the nearest 100 million. Therefore 300 million was used for the average consensus for 1AD. For 1750AD the same process was used. The estimates ranged from 629 to 961 million. The average of these numbers is 795 million. When rounded to the nearest 100 million, the average consensus for the 1750AD world population is 800 million. For 1900AD the estimates ranged from 1,550 to 1,762 million. The average for these numbers is 1,666 million. When rounded to the nearest 100 million, the average consensus for the 1900AD world population is 1,700 million. For 2000AD and 2007AD the single referenced world population number was simply rounded to the nearest 100 million. Therefore, for 2000AD the referenced number of 6,071,710,896 was rounded to 6,100 million. Likewise, for 2007AD the referenced number of 6,602,274,812 was rounded to 6,600 million.

The described averaging process was used in an effort to create uncontroversial and acceptable

WORLD POPULATION STATISTICS

world population numbers. Since all the numbers in the table have been rounded to the nearest 100 million, the numbers are actually invented and none of the numbers have been directly copied from any particular source.

Even though the working guidelines for this discussion are to use average numbers for world population statistics, the numbers used must still be valid for the purposes of this discussion. Because this discussion investigates the changes in world population over long periods of time, the accuracy of the numbers for the beginning date and the ending date must be considered. When any two numbers are mathematically manipulated, the result cannot be more accurate than the least accurate number involved. In terms of this discussion, the accuracy of the analysis for any two dates can never be better than the accuracy of the least accurate date. In this discussion the least accurate world population number is from 1AD. That number has a generally accepted accuracy of plus or minus 100 million. Therefore, the use of

THE GENERATIONS OF NOAH

population numbers which claim accuracy better than 100 million would be overstating the accuracy inherent in this discussion. For this reason all numbers used have been rounded to the nearest 100 million. Hence, the numbers used are not wrong, they are simply realistic.

Since the numbers used in this discussion have no real connection to any particular source, the argument concerning which source is better is avoided. However, for those who wish to check the numbers from multiple sources, a search of the Internet is the simplest method. In fact, anyone can verify the numbers by searching the internet for "historical world population numbers" and checking multiple secular sites. Thus, the numbers contained at various web sites can be compared to ensure that the world population numbers, used in this discussion, are "average" values. That is, they are within bounds of reasonableness.

Although many sources provide world population statistics, no recommendation is made that one

WORLD POPULATION STATISTICS

source is superior to another. No suggestion is made that any website is better than any other. No claim is made that any of the numbers used in this discussion are perfect. For the purposes of this discussion, they don't need to be. As discussed, reasonable estimates are acceptable.

Employing the general methods outlined, the following table was constructed. As indicted before, the dates chosen for the table were not arbitrary, but they also have no special significance other than they occur near the beginning, middle, or end of a century. In addition, the dates selected must have data associated with them. In other words, many sources report world population numbers for 1AD, but none report numbers for 2AD. Furthermore, the 2007AD date does not mark anything except it is the latest date that had a good world population estimate. To that point, the 2007AD number should be the most accurate in the table.

The Generations of Noah

Since this table is a collage of many modern estimates, it generally represents a consensus of secular thought concerning the population of the world since 1AD. Again, anyone can verify its "vanilla" character by simply checking a few sources. To be painfully clear, in that check these exact numbers will not necessarily be found at any particular source because they have been invented. However, since they approximate what everyone thinks are good estimates, these numbers should be agreeable to most people.

Year	Estimated World Population
1AD	300,000,000
1750AD	800,000,000
1900AD	1,700,000,000
2000AD	6,100,000,000
2007AD	6,600,000,000

WORLD POPULATION STATISTICS

All subsequent references to world population numbers will use the dates and their associated numbers listed in this table.

In retrospect the table is quite simple and the numbers are of a middle-of-the-road character. Most people would find the table to be acceptable. Thus, the original mandate has been achieved.

The construction of this table completes the second step in the overall testing process. All of the required world population data from a secular point of view has now been collected. The next and final step in the testing process is the analysis of the data.

The Generations of Noah

6

THE CHALLENGE

Thus far, the discussion has centered on the collection of data from Biblical and secular points of view. These tasks were the first two steps in the overall process. The overall data collected indicates that six people in 2319BC multiplied to 6.6 billion people in 2007AD. The third and final step is the analysis of this data. This step involves mathematics and will test the reasonableness of the Bible's numbers growing to the secular numbers during the 4,325 years of growth required by the Bible. Assuming that the secular data is correct; can the Biblical data logically coexist with it?

The Bible stipulates that Noah's flood was worldwide in scope, only six people reproduced after it, and it occurred in 2319BC. The secular data contains the world population numbers at various times in Earth's history. These numbers were intentionally taken from the last two thousand years in order to gain a consensus. Most people generally agree with the world population numbers since 1AD. However, not everyone accepts the numbers prior to 1AD. In particular, the Biblical numbers and secular numbers prior to 1AD dramatically diverge. While the Bible clearly states that a group of six people grew to the population level of 1AD in only a few thousand years, the secular point of view indicates that world population numbers during that period are much higher. Although secularists might agree that the determination of world population numbers prior to 1AD has a large component of guesswork, they generally believe the numbers a few thousand years earlier are much higher than something approximating a single digit. Because of this large disagreement between Biblical and secular numbers, some people are skeptical and believe the Biblical numbers are not realistic. In fact, some people believe the Biblical numbers are patently impossible.

The Challenge

Because of this mindset, a skeptic might challenge the Biblical statements in the following manner. The skeptic might argue, "The Earth's 2007AD population of over six billion people could not have been derived from just six people in only four or five thousand years. Millions of years, not a few thousand, are required to achieve the twenty-first century's population level." In this way the skeptic challenges every facet of the Bible's account of Noah's flood. The challenge questions the fact that Noah's flood even occurred. The challenge questions the fact that the worldwide population was decimated to a level of only eight people. The challenge questions the fact that only six people produced every human being after the year 2319BC.

The skeptic's assertion at first seems plausible. A billion is a very, very large number. It seems that a very long time would be required to produce billions of human beings. However, can this challenge be answered without resorting to Biblical or secular opinions? Can the Bible's population statements be logically tested to see if they are reasonable or not?

The answer to this question involves the modern techniques used to determine the population levels of the Earth. These techniques have been used to determine population levels for the twenty-first century. Based on well-tested and accepted mathematical formulas, these techniques produce amazingly accurate numbers. In fact, the United States Census Bureau states on their website that these same mathematical formulas are used to produce the population numbers which they publish. In turn, these mathematical formulas are based on the proven, and universally accepted, fact that populations grow according to an exponential growth rate. Through the use of empirically determined growth rates, very accurate population numbers can be determined. Moreover, these formulas have a time component so that they can be applied not only to modern times but also to time periods in the past.

THE CHALLENGE

Since populations grow according to these well-known mathematical models, the skeptics challenge can, indeed, be answered logically and objectively. The Bible's world population statements can be tested for reasonableness using mathematics. Specifically, the mathematics of exponential growth can objectively and impartially determine the answer.

The Generations of Noah

7

Exponential Growth

The mathematics of population growth is well understood and involves exponential growth. Although this chapter contains equations, it is not a lesson in mathematics. In fact, an effort to minimize mathematical terminology has been expended. Rather, it is a demonstration of the power of exponential growth.

Whenever any mathematical analysis is presented in this book, the set of equations, which support the analysis, are shaded and surrounded by a continuous border. In addition a key beginning sentence will precede the set of equations and a key ending sentence will follow the set of equations. This convention is followed so that any equations which are not essential to the flow of the text can be easily recognized. This convention also allows the mathematics to be checked by those who desire the full supporting analysis. In this way any mathematical equations which can be skipped without loss of continuity are isolated from the rest of the text.

The characteristic text and shaded area surrounding the mathematical analysis will appear as shown in the following example.

When the known values are substituted, the resulting equation can be systematically solved for the unknown value.

After the equations are solved, the following result is produced.

Exponential Growth

These key sentences and the horizontal bars across the page are used so that the mathematical parts, which are provided in the spirit of full disclosure, are easily distinguished. If the mathematics appears unintelligible, simply skip it. The context and meaning of the discussion will be maintained.

Exponential growth adheres to the following equation where P_0 is the initial population, P is the eventual population, r is the growth rate, and t is the elapsed time required for the growth.

$$P = P_0 e^{rt}$$

This equation starts with an initial population number and calculates the eventual population based on a specified growth rate over a specified amount of time. It basically determines the final population number from the doubling rate of the initial population number. The doubling rate is intrinsically embedded in the equation through the mathematical constant e, which is known as Euler's number. In addition, as a matter of convention throughout this discussion, growth rates will be expressed to a precision of five decimal places.

The exponential growth equation governs any situation where the growth is a function of the amount present. As in the example of the boy whose pay doubled each day, populations double over a characteristic length of time. For instance, the size of a bacterial colony might double every thirty minutes, or the population of a country might double every thirty years.

Although the bounds of idealized exponential growth seem to be limitless, that's not how it works in the real world. Idealized exponential growth is not natural. As previously demonstrated, a controlling factor in that growth is the growth rate, which doesn't necessarily remain constant. A bacterial colony in a Petri dish can be used to demonstrate the point. The bacterial colony might initially double its number of organisms every thirty minutes. With no consideration for any controlling factors, the size of the colony could continue to

EXPONENTIAL GROWTH

grow until it became as large as a house. In reality, however, after a few days the colony stops growing because it has exhausted the food supply in the Petri dish. The growth rate of the bacterial colony is dependent on the conditions in the Petri dish. If those conditions were controlled by adding a drop of sugar water to the Petri dish each day, a sustained growth rate over a period of time might be achieved.

Obviously, growth rates over a short period of time can be deceptive. A growth rate measured over a period of years is more realistic than a growth rate measured over a few hours. Unrealistic growth rates can produce unrealistic results. Likewise, realistic growth rates can produce realistic results. In the real world exponential growth is naturally restrained, but over a long time period those restraining influences get factored into the measured growth rate. Similarly, the multitudinous factors which affect the growth of the population of the Earth are built into its past growth rates.

THE GENERATIONS OF NOAH

The exponential growth equation can be applied to many situations such as monetary growth, bacterial growth, or human population growth. As a demonstration, it can be used to calculate the answer to the question about the boy whose pay doubled each day for a thirty day chore. The first day the boy was paid a penny, and every subsequent day his pay was doubled. During this thirty day period, his pay doubled twenty-nine times.

In order to calculate the amount of money the boy was paid on the last day using the exponential growth equation, the growth rate, r, must be determined. Since the growth rate is constant for all twenty-nine days, the parameters for a single day can be used to calculate the growth rate. During the time of one day, the pay changed from one cent to two cents.

The exponential growth equation must first be populated with the following known values.

EXPONENTIAL GROWTH

$P = 2 \text{ cents}$

$P_0 = 1 \text{ cent}$

$r = \text{unknown}$

$t = 1 \text{ day}$

When the known values are substituted, the resulting equation can be systematically solved for the unknown value.

$$P = P_0 e^{rt}$$

$$2 \text{ cents} = (1 \text{ cent}) \, e^{r(1 \text{ day})}$$

Solving for r gives the following results.

$$2 = e^{r \text{ day}}$$

$$\ln(2) = \ln(e^{r \text{ day}})$$

$$\ln(2) = r \text{ day}$$

$r \, day = ln(2)$

$r = ln(2) \, / \, day$

$r = 0.69315 \, / \, day$

$r = 0.69315 \text{ per } day$

After the equations are solved, the following result is produced. The daily growth rate for this example is 0.69315 or more precisely ln(2). The notation ln(2) indicates the natural logarithm of 2. This value can be determined using a modern calculator. For this particular case the exact growth rate of ln(2) can be used; therefore, it does not need to be rounded to five decimal places. This growth rate can be used to calculate the final payment that the boy received.

EXPONENTIAL GROWTH

On the first day the boy had one cent. During the thirty days of work, that penny experienced a growth rate of ln(2) for twenty-nine days.

Again, the exponential growth equation must be populated with the known values, which now includes the calculated value for r. Since the eventual pay is being calculated, P is the unknown.

$P = unknown$
$P_0 = 1\ cent$
$r = ln(2)\,/\,day = 0.69315\,/\,day$
$t = 29\ days$

When the known values are substituted, the resulting equation can be systematically solved for the unknown value.

$$P = P_0 e^{rt}$$

$$P = (1\ cent)\ e^{(ln2\,/\,day)(29\ days)}$$

Solving for P gives the following results.

$$P = e^{(\ln 2)(29)} \text{ cents}$$

$$P = 536870912 \text{ cents}$$

$$P = \$5,368,709.12$$

After the equations are solved, the following result is produced. Based on the calculated daily growth rate, the amount of money the boy was paid on the last day was $5,368,709.12.

The fact that the boy gets paid over $5 million dollars for his last day of work is quite startling. Of course, this fictitious story presents an idealized situation. In reality no one gets paid that way. Typically, a person gets paid the same amount if the same amount of work is done. In a more realistic scenario, a person might be paid interest

EXPONENTIAL GROWTH

by a bank based on how much money is in a savings account at the end of each day. In such a case, the person might deposit or withdraw money at any time. Furthermore, these deposits and withdrawals vary in magnitude; hence the interest paid could vary from day to day based on the variable amount in the account.

Similarly, populations of people do not increase in size unrestrained. Nor do they increase at constant rates. Many negative effects, including diseases, disasters, and wars, have an impact on population growth. In addition, many positive effects, including medical innovations, eras of beneficial climate, and times of peace, have an impact on population growth. Such events create a continuously changing population growth rate for the planet Earth. Although such effects definitely change the growth rate, populations still grow exponentially according to the equation. The point is that constant growth rates in the real world simply do not exist over extended periods of time. For this reason many population growth studies use the "average" growth rate over a specified period of time.

Obviously, the growth rate is an important part of the equation. In particular, it can be negative or positive. When the growth rate is less than zero, the population is decreasing; when it is greater than zero, the population is increasing. Not unexpectedly, when it is zero, the population is constant and has zero growth. This effect can be seen by solving the exponential growth equation while the growth rate, r, is zero.

The exponential growth equation must be populated with the following values. In this case r is the only known value.

$$P = unknown$$
$$P_0 = unknown$$
$$r = 0$$
$$t = unknown$$

EXPONENTIAL GROWTH

When this one known value is substituted into the exponential growth equation, the resulting equation can be systematically solved.

$$P = P_0 e^{rt}$$

$$P = P_0 e^{0(t)}$$

$$P = P_0 e^{0}$$

Since e^0 equals one, the equation can be reduced.

$$P = P_0$$

After the equations are solved, the following result is produced. When the growth rate is zero, the size of the final population is equal to the size of the beginning population. This result is true for all time periods.

THE GENERATIONS OF NOAH

In addition, the equations show more information about the growth rate number. The larger the growth rate number, the more rapidly the population increases. In the example of the boy whose pay doubled each day, the growth rate was calculated to be 0.69315 or ln(2). However, if his pay had tripled each day, the daily growth rate would have been 1.09861 or ln(3). Likewise, if the boy's pay had quadrupled each day, the daily growth rate would have been 1.38629 or ln(4), which is twice the magnitude of the growth rate when the boy's pay was doubled.

Another interesting example can be cited. World population counters are very popular, and many can be found on the Internet. They display the current population of the world. However, they do not display the actual world population count. Instead, they simply increment the estimated population by a predetermined amount every second or so. This increment is based on the calculated average growth rate for Earth's

EXPONENTIAL GROWTH

population. The counter looks very dramatic, but it is just adding to the total a calculated number, which is based on the average growth rate.

The exponential growth equation is very powerful. In fact, the United States Census Bureau's website, **http://www.census.gov/ipc/www/idb/worldpop.html**, specifically states that this same equation is used for their calculations.

THE GENERATIONS OF NOAH

8

TEST FOR REASONABLENESS

Obviously, testing the Biblical population numbers involves exponential growth, but exactly how should that test be performed and what are the parameters for its success or failure? The goal is to determine if the Biblical numbers are reasonable or not. Mathematics will be the judge of the test, but how can the term "reasonable" be mathematically defined?

As stated previously, the secular world population numbers from 1AD and after are assumed to be correct. The table of world population numbers has the specific dates of 1AD, 1750AD, 1900AD, 2000AD, and 2007AD. Using the exponential growth equation, the growth rates from one of these dates to the other can be calculated. These calculated growth rates will be average yearly growth rates from the first date to the second date.

THE GENERATIONS OF NOAH

Therefore, for the purposes of this discussion, good average growth rates can be calculated using the numbers in the table. Arbitrarily, the growth rates will be calculated to the end date of 2007AD. This is done to maximize the time periods over which the calculations will be performed and to ensure that the ending date for all calculations is from the twenty-first century, which has better numbers. In other words, the calculated growth rates will be from 1AD to 20007AD, from 1750AD to 2007AD, from 1900AD to 2007AD, and from 2000AD to 2007AD.

After a growth rate is calculated, that growth rate will be applied to the unknown period of time prior to 1AD. Specifically, that growth rate will be used to calculate the number of years required to go back from the 300 million world population level to six people. Because four different growth rates will be calculated, four different answers will be calculated. All four sets of calculations will provide a calculated estimate for the date of Noah's flood. In turn, each

TEST FOR REASONABLENESS

calculated date will be judged for its reasonableness.

Since exact numbers are not available for these tests, the tests cannot be exact. However, value can still be derived from their performance. If growth rates from times that have reasonable population numbers are calculated and then those growth rates are applied to times which have no numbers, a test for reasonableness of the Biblical numbers can be performed. Such strategies are often employed to predict future world population numbers. A moment of thought begs the question: "How can a future population number be predicted when the growth rate for the intervening time period has not happened yet?" The simple answer is that growth rates are projected to the future event. One example is a world population calculator which can take a future year and calculate the world population for that year. The answer it produces is an estimate based on current or past growth rates, which are applied to future years. The actual future growth rate is not known;

however, the future growth rate is assumed to be a function of known historical growth rates. Based on that assumption, the world population calculator estimates future population numbers. This same strategy will be used in the calculations for the date of Noah's flood. However, it will be applied in reverse. Instead of estimating future world populations, past populations will be estimated. In other words, modern growth rates will be used to calculate possible population numbers in the recent past.

This simple investigation of exponential growth should determine if the Biblical population statements are reasonable or not. Mathematics will be an impartial judge and show if the population numbers are reasonable. Since the rate of world population change was probably not the same before and after 1AD, the answer produced will be a ballpark figure. However, as stated, the goal is to show reasonableness or not.

TEST FOR REASONABLENESS

The question then becomes, "How can reasonableness be determined for these estimated dates?" Obviously, if a calculated date for Noah's flood is in a reasonable neighborhood of 2319BC, then that calculated date would be reasonable. However, how can a "reasonable neighborhood" be quantified?

One way to determine a reasonable quantitative boundary is to allow one order of magnitude. This method is often applied in ordinary circumstances. For example, if the target number were twenty, the next order of magnitude would be ten times twenty, or two-hundred. Similarly, if the order of magnitude were in the thousands, the next higher order of magnitude would be in the ten-thousands. In the case of Noah's flood, the analysis ranges from 2319BC to 2007AD, a period of 4,325 years. The next order of magnitude would be ten times that, or 43,250 years. In these terms the upper limit for the next order of magnitude for Noah's flood date of 2319BC would be 45,569BC. This date is the sum of 2,319 and 43,250. Therefore, if this boundary condition were used, the calculated date for Noah's flood would not be reasonable if it were older than 45,569BC.

Another way to determine a reasonable quantitative boundary is to take a percentage of the expected value. Most people would accept 10% as a reasonable percentage because then they would get 90% of what they expected. An even tighter, and more acceptable, boundary would be 1%. As an example, if someone owed a debt of $100, they would be pleased if the debt were reduced to 1% of the original amount. With a 1% expectation, they would only be required to repay $1. Since the skeptic believes millions of years are required to achieve the twenty-first century world population numbers, a conservative boundary would be 1% of a million, or 10,000 years. In that case the 2319BC date would be reasonable if the calculated date was within 10,000 years of 2319BC. In other words, if the calculated date was less than 12,319BC, the calculated date would be reasonable.

TEST FOR REASONABLENESS

Several methods for defining a reasonable calculation have been explored. The most stringent was the 10,000-year limit; therefore that quantitative neighborhood will be used. For the purposes of this discussion "reasonableness" will be defined as follows. If the mathematics shows that a calculated date for Noah's flood is within 10,000 years of the Biblical date, 2319BC, then the Biblical date for Noah's flood is reasonable.

THE GENERATIONS OF NOAH

9

TEST FROM 1AD TO 2007AD

Having defined the testing procedure, the third and final step in the overall process, which is the analysis of the collected data, can begin. As stated previously, this step will test the reasonableness of the Bible's numbers growing to the secular numbers during the amount of time specified by the Bible. Because the Biblical data is being tested, throughout this procedure the secular data is assumed to be correct.

The first test will involve the collected data from 1AD to 2007AD. As might be expected, the initial task in this test is the calculation of the average yearly rate of growth from 1AD to 2007AD. This rate will have negatives, such as, calamities, diseases, and famines, and positives, such as, population spurts, already factored into it. This growth rate is based on the longest period of

THE GENERATIONS OF NOAH

human history for which reasonable world population numbers are available. As previously stated the world population for 1AD was 300 million and 6.6 billion for 2007AD. Also, this period of time spans 2006 years of population growth.

The well-established exponential growth equation, where P_0 is the initial population, P is the eventual population, r is the growth rate, and t is the elapsed time required for the growth, will be used.

$$P = P_0 e^{rt}$$

This equation must be populated with the following known values.

$$P = 6,600,000,000$$
$$P_0 = 300,000,000$$
$$r = unknown$$
$$t = 2006 \text{ years}$$

When the known values are substituted, the resulting equation can be systematically solved for the unknown value.

TEST FROM 1AD TO 2007AD

$P = P_0 e^{rt}$

$6{,}600{,}000{,}000 = (300{,}000{,}000)\, e^{rt}$

$6{,}600{,}000{,}000 = (300{,}000{,}000)\, e^{r\,(2006\ years)}$

Since the growth rate, *r*, is the only unknown, *r* can be calculated.

$6{,}600{,}000{,}000 = (300{,}000{,}000)\, e^{r\,(2006\ years)}$

$6{,}600{,}000{,}000 / 300{,}000{,}000 = e^{r\,(2006\ years)}$

$22 = e^{r\,(2006\ years)}$

$ln(22) = ln(e^{r\,(2006\ years)})$

$ln(22) = r(2006\ years)$

$r(2006\ years) = ln(22)$

$$r = \ln(22) / (2006 \text{ years})$$

$$r = 3.0910 / (2006 \text{ years})$$

$$r = 0.00154 / \text{year}$$

$$r = 0.00154 \text{ per year}$$

After the equations are solved, the following result is produced. The calculated average yearly growth rate is 0.00154. This yearly growth rate is the overall growth rate from 1AD to 2007AD. This is most definitely not the human growth rate for the period before 1AD since growth rates fluctuate over time. For example, it contains the growth spurt of the baby boomer generation of the late twentieth century. It, also, contains the fourteenth century and seventeenth century Black Death effects that certainly slowed the rate by decimating the world

TEST FROM 1AD TO 2007AD

population. But since it is a real rate for a 2006-year period, which is the longest period of reasonable data available, it is sufficient to test reasonableness.

The next step is to use the calculated growth rate to find the date when the population was six people. That is, the calculated growth rate can be used to find the number of years required to go from six people to 300 million in 1AD. The same exponential growth equation is used.

$$P = P_0 e^{rt}$$

This equation must be populated with the following known values.

P = $300,000,000$
P_0 = 6
r = $0.00154 / year$
t = $unknown$

THE GENERATIONS OF NOAH

When the known values are substituted, the resulting equation can be systematically solved for the unknown value.

$$P = P_0 e^{rt}$$

$$300{,}000{,}000 = (6)\, e^{rt}$$

$$300{,}000{,}000 = (6)\, e^{(0.00154/year)\, t}$$

$$300{,}000{,}000 / 6 = e^{(0.00154/year)\, t}$$

$$50{,}000{,}000 = e^{(0.00154)\, t}$$

Since the elapsed time, **t**, is the only unknown, **t** can be calculated.

$$50{,}000{,}000 = e^{(0.00154/year)\, t}$$

$$\ln(50{,}000{,}000) = \ln(e^{(0.00154/year)\, t})$$

TEST FROM 1AD TO 2007AD

$$ln(50,000,000) = (0.00154/year)\ t$$

$$17.7275 = (0.00154/year)\ t$$

$$(0.00154/year)\ t = 17.7275$$

$$t = 17.7275 / (0.00154/year)$$

$$t = (17.7275 / 0.00154)\ years$$

$$t = 11,511\ years$$

After the equations are solved, the following result is produced. Given the assumptions of the calculation, the date of the flood is estimated to be 11,511 years prior to 1AD. Since the year 0AD does not exist, the year 1AD was preceded by 1BC. When 11,511 years are counted backwards from 1AD, the estimated year is 11,511BC. Simple mathematics proves that millions of years are not required to reach twenty-first century population levels. In fact, tens of thousands of years are not even required. Using a real human historical growth rate, less than 14,000 years are required to produce the twenty-first century's population from six people. Also, since the Bible states that people immediately after the flood lived much longer than people after 1AD, the growth rate according to the Bible should be higher. Therefore, from a Biblical point of view the actual date of the flood should be less than 11,511BC.

The test for reasonableness can now be completed. If 11,511BC is within 10,000 years of the Biblical date for Noah's flood, then the Biblical date is reasonable. Since 11,511BC is 9,192 years greater than 2319BC, the Biblical date has been shown to be reasonable.

10

TEST FROM 1750AD TO 2007AD

Objectivity demands that more than one historical growth rate be used. The first growth rate calculated was over the longest period that had reasonable data. The next longest period from the collected data is from 1750AD to 2007AD. This period of time spans 257 years of population growth.

As previously stated, the world population data for 1750AD was 800 million and for 2007AD the population was 6.6 billion. As before, the growth rate from 1750AD to 2007AD must be calculated using the exponential growth equation.

$$P = P_0 e^{rt}$$

This equation must be populated with the following known values.

THE GENERATIONS OF NOAH

$P = 6{,}600{,}000{,}000$
$P_0 = 800{,}000{,}000$
$r = unknown$
$t = 257 \; years$

When the known values are substituted, the resulting equation can be systematically solved for the unknown value.

$$P = P_0 \, e^{rt}$$

$$6{,}600{,}000{,}000 = (800{,}000{,}000) \, e^{rt}$$

$$6{,}600{,}000{,}000 = (800{,}000{,}000) \, e^{r(106 \; years)}$$

Since the growth rate, r, is the only unknown, r can be calculated.

$$6{,}500{,}000{,}000 = (800{,}000{,}000) \, e^{r(257 \; years)}$$

TEST FROM 1750AD TO 2007AD

$6,600,000,000 / 800,000,000 = e^{r(257 \text{ years})}$

$8.25 = e^{r(257 \text{ years})}$

$\ln(8.25) = \ln(e^{r(257 \text{ years})})$

$\ln(8.25) = r(257 \text{ years})$

$r(257 \text{ years}) = \ln(8.25)$

$r = \ln(8.25) / (257 \text{ years})$

$r = 2.1102 / (257 \text{ years})$

$r = (2.1102 / 257) / \text{year}$

$r = 0.00821 / \text{year}$

$r = 0.00821$ per year

THE GENERATIONS OF NOAH

After the equations are solved, the following result is produced. The calculated average yearly growth rate is 0.00821. Again, this growth rate is not the growth rate before 1AD, but it is a real and accurate human growth rate from 1750AD to 2007AD. It is being used only to test reasonableness.

The same basic exponential growth equation is used to calculate the years.

$$P = P_0 e^{rt}$$

This equation must be populated with the following known values.

$P = 300,000,000$
$P_0 = 6$
$r = 0.00821 \,/\, year$
$t = unknown$

When the known values are substituted, the resulting equation can be systematically solved for the unknown value.

TEST FROM 1750AD TO 2007AD

$$P = P_0 e^{rt}$$

$$300{,}000{,}000 = (6) e^{rt}$$

$$300{,}000{,}000 = (6) e^{(0.00821/year) t}$$

Since the elapsed time, *t*, is the only unknown, *t* can be calculated.

$$300{,}000{,}000 = (6) e^{(0.00821/year) t}$$

$$300{,}000{,}000 / 6 = e^{(0.00821/year) t}$$

$$50{,}000{,}000 = e^{(0.00821/year) t}$$

$$\ln(50{,}000{,}000) = \ln(e^{(0.00821/year) t})$$

$$\ln(50{,}000{,}000) = (0.00821/year) t$$

$$17.7275 = (0.00821/year) t$$

$$(0.00821/year) t = 17.7275$$

THE GENERATIONS OF NOAH

$$t = 17.7275 / (0.00821 / year)$$

$$t = (17.7275 / 0.00821) \; years$$

$$t = 2159 \; years$$

After the equations are solved, the following result is produced. Using modern and accurate growth rate numbers, the date for the flood is estimated to be 2,159 years prior to 1AD, or 2159BC. This date was calculated using the positive and negative growth fluctuations from 1750AD to 2007AD. Although many positive and negative factors are built into this estimate, it is calculated based on real historical events. Such events are common to real human populations and should add credibility to the estimate.

This calculated estimate of 2159BC for the date of Noah's flood is extremely close to the Biblical date of 2319BC. In fact, the two dates are only 160 years apart. Obviously, the test for reasonableness has been satisfied since 2159BC is within 10,000

TEST FROM 1750AD TO 2007AD

years of the Biblical date for Noah's flood of 2319BC. Therefore, according to this test, the Biblical date is reasonable.

Again, simple mathematics proves that a real, long-range human growth rate only requires a few thousand years to produce the twenty-first century's population of billions.

The Generations of Noah

11

TEST FROM **1900AD** TO **2007AD**

The next span of time to be examined is from 1900AD to 2007AD. This is the first time span in this discussion with beginning and ending dates that fall in the twentieth century or later. As already determined, population estimates for this period are generally better than estimates previous to the twentieth century. Hence, the calculated growth rates should also be more accurate. The period of time from 1900AD to 2007AD spans 107 years of population growth.

As previously stated, the world population numbers for 1900AD was 1.7 billion and for 2007AD the number was 6.6 billion. Again, the growth rate from 1900AD to 2007AD must be calculated using the exponential growth equation.

$$P = P_0\, e^{rt}$$

THE GENERATIONS OF NOAH

This equation must be populated with the following known values.

$$P = 6{,}600{,}000{,}000$$
$$P_0 = 1{,}700{,}000{,}000$$
$$r = unknown$$
$$t = 107 \ years$$

When the known values are substituted, the resulting equation can be systematically solved for the unknown value.

$$P = P_0 e^{rt}$$

$$6{,}600{,}000{,}000 = (1{,}700{,}000{,}000)\, e^{rt}$$

$$6{,}600{,}000{,}000 = (1{,}700{,}000{,}000)\, e^{r\,(107\ years)}$$

Since the growth rate, r, is the only unknown, r can be calculated.

TEST FROM 1900AD TO 2007AD

$6{,}600{,}000{,}000 = (1{,}700{,}000{,}000)\ e^{r\,(107\ years)}$

$6{,}600{,}000{,}000\ /\ 1{,}700{,}000{,}000 = e^{r\,(107\ years)}$

$3.882 = e^{r\,(107\ years)}$

$\ln(3.882) = \ln(e^{r\,(107\ years)})$

$\ln(3.882) = r(107\ years)$

$r(107\ years) = \ln(3.882)$

$r = \ln(3.882)\ /\ (107\ years)$

$r = 1.3564\ /\ (107\ years)$

$r = (1.3564\ /\ 107)\ /\ year$

$r = 0.01268\ /\ year$

$r = 0.01268\ per\ year$

THE GENERATIONS OF NOAH

After the equations are solved, the following result is produced. The calculated average yearly growth rate is 0.01268. Clearly, this growth rate is not the growth rate before 1AD, but it is a real and accurate human growth rate from 1900AD to 2007AD. It is being used only to test reasonableness.

The same basic exponential growth equation is used to calculate the years.

$$P = P_0 e^{rt}$$

This equation must be populated with the following known values.

$$P = 300,000,000$$
$$P_0 = 6$$
$$r = 0.01268 / year$$
$$t = unknown$$

When the known values are substituted, the resulting equation can be systematically solved for the unknown value.

TEST FROM 1900AD TO 2007AD

$$P = P_0 e^{rt}$$

$$300{,}000{,}000 = (6)\, e^{rt}$$

$$300{,}000{,}000 = (6)\, e^{(0.01268/year)\, t}$$

Since the elapsed time, *t*, is the only unknown, *t* can be calculated.

$$300{,}000{,}000 = (6)\, e^{(0.01268/year)\, t}$$

$$300{,}000{,}000 / 6 = e^{(0.01268/year)\, t}$$

$$50{,}000{,}000 = e^{(0.01268/year)\, t}$$

$$ln(\,50{,}000{,}000\,) = ln(\, e^{(0.01268/year)\, t}\,)$$

$$ln(\,50{,}000{,}000\,) = (0.01268/year)\, t$$

$$17.7275 = (0.01268/year)\, t$$

THE GENERATIONS OF NOAH

> *(0.01268 / year) t = 17.7275*
>
> *t = 17.7275 / (0.01268 / year)*
>
> *t = (17.7275 / 0.01268) years*
>
> *t = 1398 years*

After the equations are solved, the following result is produced. Using modern and accurate growth rate numbers, the date for the flood is estimated to be 1,398 years prior to 1AD, or 1398BC. This date was calculated using the growth rate effect of the twentieth century. It contains the effects of the high reproduction period of the baby boomer generation after World War II and the most efficacious period of human medicine since 1AD. These positive effects should move the calculated date for Noah's flood closer to the present age. Based upon this

TEST FROM 1900AD TO 2007AD

argument, the actual date of the flood should be greater than 1398BC.

In any case, the Biblical date for Noah's flood is by definition reasonable. That is, 1398BC is within 10,000 years of the Biblical date of 2319BC. In fact, the difference between 1398BC and 2319BC is only 921 years. Again, simple mathematics proves that a real, long-range human growth rate only requires a few thousand years to produce the twenty-first century's population.

THE GENERATIONS OF NOAH

12

TEST FROM 2000AD TO 2007AD

What would the estimated date for the flood be if the actual growth rate from 2000AD to 2007AD were used? This time period spans seven years of population growth. As previously stated, the world population number for 2000AD was 6.1 billion and for 2007AD the number was 6.6 billion.

The growth rate from 2000AD to 2007AD must be calculated using the exponential growth equation.

$$P = P_0 e^{rt}$$

This equation must be populated with the following known values.

$$P = 6,600,000,000$$
$$P_0 = 6,100,000,000$$
$$r = unknown$$

THE GENERATIONS OF NOAH

$t = 7\ years$

When the known values are substituted, the resulting equation can be systematically solved for the unknown value.

$$P = P_0 e^{rt}$$

$$6{,}600{,}000{,}000 = (6{,}100{,}000{,}000)\ e^{rt}$$

$$6{,}600{,}000{,}000 = (6{,}100{,}000{,}000)\ e^{r\,(7\ years)}$$

Since the growth rate, r, is the only unknown, r can be calculated.

$$6{,}600{,}000{,}000 = (6{,}100{,}000{,}000)\ e^{r\,(7\ years)}$$

$$6{,}600{,}000{,}000\ /\ 6{,}100{,}000{,}000 = e^{r\,(7\ years)}$$

$$1.082 = e^{r\,(7\ years)}$$

TEST FROM 2000AD TO 2007AD

$$ln(1.082) = ln(e^{r(7\,years)})$$

$$ln(1.082) = r(7\,years)$$

$$r(7\,years) = ln(1.082)$$

$$r = ln(1.082) / (7\,years)$$

$$r = 0.0788 / (7\,years)$$

$$r = 0.01126 / year$$

$$r = 0.01126\ per\ year$$

After the equations are solved, the following result is produced. The calculated average yearly growth rate from 2000AD to 2007AD is 0.01126.

Now that the growth rate is known, the time required for six people to reproduce to the 1AD

The Generations of Noah

population of 300 million can be calculated. The same exponential growth equation is used.

$$P = P_0 e^{rt}$$

This equation must be populated with the following known values.

P = 300,000,000
P_0 = 6
r = 0.01126 / year
t = unknown

When the known values are substituted, the resulting equation can be systematically solved for the unknown value.

$$P = P_0 e^{rt}$$

$$300,000,000 = (6) e^{rt}$$

TEST FROM 2000AD TO 2007AD

$300{,}000{,}000 = (6)\, e^{(0.01126/year)\, t}$

Since the elapsed time, *t*, is the only unknown, *t* can be calculated.

$300{,}000{,}000 = (6)\, e^{(0.01126/year)\, t}$

$300{,}000{,}000 / 6 = e^{(0.01126/year)\, t}$

$50{,}000{,}000 = e^{(0.01126/year)\, t}$

$\ln(50{,}000{,}000) = \ln(e^{(0.01126/year)\, t})$

$\ln(50{,}000{,}000) = (0.01126/year)\, t$

$17.7275 = (0.01126/year)\, t$

$(0.01126/year)\, t = 17.7275$

$t = 17.7275 / (0.01126/year)$

$t = (17.7275 / 0.01126)\ years$

THE GENERATIONS OF NOAH

$$t = 1{,}574 \ years$$

After the equations are solved, the following result is produced. Using recent and arguably the most accurate growth rate numbers available, the date for the flood is estimated to be 1,574 years prior to 1AD, or 1574BC.

Again, simple mathematics proves that only a few thousand years are required to produce the twenty-first century's population. In fact, according to this calculation, six people can grow to 6.6 billion people in 3,580 years.

The calculated estimate of 1574BC for Noah's flood is remarkably close to the Biblical date of 2319BC. In fact, they are only 745 years apart. Still, no particular significance can be assigned to this fact. Because the growth rate for 2319BC and all the years from then to 1AD are unknown, no

TEST FROM 2000AD TO 2007AD

exact calculation can be made. However, the growth rates that are known can be used to test for reasonableness. Moreover, the growth rate from 2000AD to 2007AD is not debatable. It is derived from accurate modern world population numbers which are not disputed. Nevertheless, this growth rate cannot be proved to be the same as the growth rate from the date of Noah's flood to 1AD. In fact, it most probably is not. However, when this growth rate is used in a test for reasonableness, the resulting calculated date shows that the Biblical date meets every condition for reasonableness. Most pointedly, the calculated date for Noah's flood of 1574BC is within 10,000 years of the Biblical date of 2319BC; therefore, according to this calculation, 2319BC is reasonable.

THE GENERATIONS OF NOAH

13

CONFIRMING THE WORD

A series of real historical human world population growth rates produced dates relatively close to the Biblical dating for Noah's flood. In fact, calculated dates, which occur before and after the Biblical flood date, can be demonstrated.

As emphasized, the numbers used in the calculations are not hypothetical. They are real numbers. Specifically, actual, verifiable growth rates from a few thousand years after 1AD were applied to a few thousand years before 1AD. This methodology certainly cannot be used to calculate the real population before 1AD, but it can be used to provide a reasonable estimate.

Furthermore, the growth rates were not taken from small time spans and then applied to immense time spans. That is, the population growth rate for March 5, 1955, was not applied to the preceding 65 million years. That kind of sophistry was not employed. Nor was an exhaustive search for a "magic" growth rate initiated until one, which agreed with the initial proposition, was found. Many historical growth rates were used over logical time spans. Moreover, each test produced the same result. Each calculated date was within 10,000 years of the Biblical date for Noah's flood; and therefore, the Biblical date was found to be reasonable in every test.

At this point in the discussion, the evidence clearly supports the plausibility of the Biblical account of Noah's flood. In other words, each of the different time spans tested has failed to disprove the Biblical statements concerning Noah's flood. The Biblical date has been shown to be reasonable in terms of the Earth's historical population record. Mathematics has confirmed the reasonableness of the word of the Bible.

CONFIRMING THE WORD

Even though the mathematical results do not provide any reason to doubt the word of God, someone might argue that the definition used for reasonableness was a bit arbitrary. To quiet any such gainsaying, another point can be made.

Most people can agree that 300 million people in 1AD grew to 6.6 billion people in 2007AD because those numbers are part of the "accepted" historical record. Therefore, the challenge is actually reduced to the question, "Is it reasonable for six people in 2319BC to grow to 300 million in 1AD?" Having persevered through the preceding discussion and having constructed a list of real world population growth rates, the term "reasonable" can now be more accurately defined. The growth is reasonable if the growth rate is reasonable. The growth rate is reasonable if it is higher than the lowest previously discussed historical growth rate and it is lower than the highest historical growth rate. In other words, the Bible growth rate is reasonable if it compares well to actual historical growth rates. The following table shows the historical growth rates, which were

THE GENERATIONS OF NOAH

used in this discussion, from the lowest to the highest.

Time Span	Growth Rate
1AD to 2007AD	**0.00154**
1750AD to 2007AD	0.00821
2000AD to 2007AD	0.01126
1900AD to 2007AD	**0.01268**

As can be seen in this growth rate table, the lowest historical world population growth rate is 0.00154 and the highest is 0.01268. If the growth rate based on the Biblical date for Noah's flood is higher than 0.00154 and it is lower than 0.01268, then by this new definition the Biblical date for Noah's flood is reasonable.

Since the Biblical growth rate from 2319BC to 1AD can be calculated using the same techniques used

CONFIRMING THE WORD

for the previous secular examples, the answer can be quickly determined. In simple terms, the Biblical growth rate must be calculated and then it must be compared to the historical growth rates in the table.

The growth rate that would be required for six people to grow to 300 million from 2319BC to 1AD can be calculated since all other values in the exponential growth equation are known. In this case the value for t would be the number of growth years from 2319BC to 1AD. That number is equal to 2319 years. The calculation begins with the familiar form of the exponential growth equation.

$$P = P_0 e^{rt}$$

This equation must be populated with the following known values.

$$\begin{aligned} P &= 300{,}000{,}000 \\ P_0 &= 6 \\ r &= unknown \\ t &= 2319 \ years \end{aligned}$$

THE GENERATIONS OF NOAH

When the known values are substituted, the resulting equation can be systematically solved for the unknown value.

$$P = P_0 e^{rt}$$

$$300{,}000{,}000 = (6) e^{rt}$$

$$300{,}000{,}000 = (6) e^{r(2319 \text{ years})}$$

Since the growth rate, r, is the only unknown, r can be calculated.

$$300{,}000{,}000 = (6) e^{r(2319 \text{ years})}$$

$$300{,}000{,}000 / 6 = e^{r(2319 \text{ years})}$$

$$50{,}000{,}000 = e^{r(2319 \text{ years})}$$

$$\ln(50{,}000{,}000) = \ln(e^{r(2319 \text{ years})})$$

CONFIRMING THE WORD

$$ln(50,000,000) = r(2319 \text{ years})$$

$$r(2319 \text{ years}) = ln(50,000,000)$$

$$r = ln(50,000,000) / (2319 \text{ years})$$

$$r = 17.72753 / (2319 \text{ years})$$

$$r = 0.00764 / \text{year}$$

$$r = 0.00764 \text{ per year}$$

After the equations are solved, the following result is produced. The calculated average yearly growth rate from 2319BC to 1AD with a predetermined population increase from six to 300 million is 0.00764. This growth rate is very close to the real historical growth rate from 1750AD to 2007AD. That world population growth rate was 0.00821.

THE GENERATIONS OF NOAH

When the growth rate table is updated with this new data, the following table is produced.

Time Span	Growth Rate
1AD to 2007AD	**0.00154**
2319BC to 1AD	**0.00764**
1750AD to 2007AD	0.00821
2000AD to 2007AD	0.01126
1900AD to 2007AD	**0.01268**

The shaded row in the table shows the growth rate from the Biblical date of Noah's flood to 1AD. This value is in the middle of all the "acceptable" historical values for the world's population growth. Since this growth rate is higher than the lowest growth rate discussed, and it is lower than the highest growth rate, it has been proved unequivocally that it is as probable as any of the other historically recorded growth rates. It is not just reasonable; it is completely consistent with the Earth's recorded population statistics. It has, in fact, been shown to be realistic.

To be clear, mathematics has not proven the Biblical date for Noah's flood, but it has confirmed the reasonableness of it. As has been shown, the Biblical date cannot be summarily dismissed because of population arguments.

Just as the twelve disciples confirmed the word when Jesus sent them into the whole Earth to spread the gospel, modern mathematics has confirmed the reasonableness of the Bible's claims concerning Noah's flood.

> Mark 16:19-20
> [19]So then after the Lord had spoken unto them, he was received up into heaven, and sat on the right hand of God. [20]And they went forth, and preached every where, the Lord working with *them*, and **confirming the word**…

The Generations of Noah

Christians confirm the word of God. They do not try to find loopholes and invent special dogma. They do not try to rewrite or misinterpret the unobstructed history recorded in the Bible. They work with Jesus. The Holy Spirit guides each Christian perfectly into the will of God. A Christian enjoys the company of God's Spirit and seeks His continuous presence.

Unfortunately, in the secular world the Bible has become the subject of endless debates. Such debates sometimes take on the character of a pretentious game. However, the Bible is not something to be frivolously debated. It is a touchstone for truth. When God said that Noah's flood was worldwide and it destroyed all the people on the Earth except for Noah and his family, why must anyone question it? They may as well be arguing with God.

Some believe that Noah's flood was not possible. They can't comprehend it because it doesn't fit their scientific mindset. They incorrectly believe

CONFIRMING THE WORD

that God is so feeble that He can't do what He says. They deny the truth of what God said He did, and they deny the truth of what God said He will do. In their denial of the past global flood, they deny the coming global storm. Nevertheless, no longer does a reason exist to reject the Biblical account because the numbers make no sense. As shown the numbers do make sense. As a witness against all of the unfaithful, the Bible's truth, and in particular its account of Noah's flood, stands unchanged.

Because modern mathematics has provided support for the Biblical account of Noah's flood, a Christian's faith in that account cannot be negated or invalidated by population arguments. Modern population growth patterns support rather than refute the Biblical account. Six people can grow to a population of billions in a few thousand years. In this modern world a Christian's faith is reasonable.

The Generations of Noah

And so, as the world debates, the Bible steadfastly proclaims that Noah's flood happened just as it was spoken by God.

More information and additional copies of this book may be obtained at the following website.

www. BibleCite. com

www.ingramcontent.com/pod-product-compliance
Lightning Source LLC
Chambersburg PA
CBHW030943090426
42737CB00007B/526